TONIA TODMAN'S
Wreaths & Garlands
BOOK

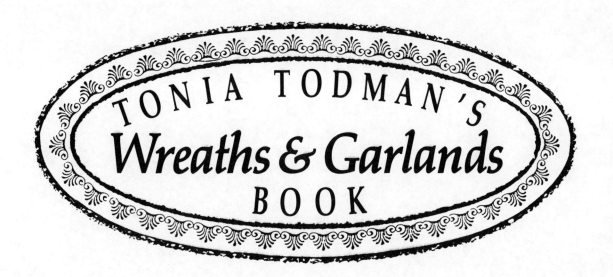

TONIA TODMAN'S
Wreaths & Garlands
BOOK

First published in 1992
Prepared by Sally Milner Publishing Pty Ltd
for Gary Allen Pty Ltd
9 Cooper Street
Smithfield NSW 2164

© Todman Services Pty Ltd, 1992

Production by Sylvana Scannapiego,
Island Graphics
Design by Gatya Kelly
Layout by Shirley Peters
Photography by Andrew Elton
Illustrations by Angela Downes
Typeset by Shirley Peters
Printed in Australia by Impact Printing, Melbourne

National Library of Australia
Cataloguing-in-Publication data:

Todman, Tonia.
    Tonia Todman's wreaths and garlands book.

ISBN 1 86351 0966

    1. Wreaths. I. Title. II. Title: Wreaths and garlands book.

745.92

Contents

Introduction

I know many of you are frustrated florists – just as I am. Flowers and other natural offerings, whether fresh or dried, are such a delight to have around us that the effect of their presence in our homes is uplifting and joyful. Flowers need not be grand in their arrangement to be noticed; indeed it is often the simplest arrangements that bring most happiness. Flowers act as visual celebratory signals to your visitors and family; they tell of your welcoming ways, of your recognition of the seasons, of a joyous Christmas, or they can simply show how you've personalised your surroundings in the most delightful way.

What better way to decorate your home than with wreaths and garlands. You may be familiar with wreaths as they've become a desirable floral accessory to any decor over the past few years, but garlands are catching up fast, and are now being used in most attractive ways for all manner of reasons.

If you have never worked with floral materials in this way before, you are in for a treat, for there is so much you can do that is simple and easily accomplished. Those of you who are familiar with this lovely craft will find some fresh ideas on trimming wreaths and garlands, drying and preserving flowers and unusual ways with using found objects.

Getting started

The materials needed for making wreaths and garlands are quite simple. So much of what you use can be collected from nature, and the tools needed to transform these natural treasures into greater things of beauty are few. Compromises are most acceptable; you don't have to own the best tools, your workbench does not have to be custom made, and your fastening methods can be as simple as using wires of different gauges, or even string. However, throughout the book I will be endeavouring to tell you of the ideal equipment and materials to gather around you, and the best time-honoured ways of making wreaths and garlands.

Tools

Secateurs

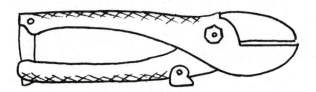

If you only can afford to purchase a few tools, you will gain long term benefits by owning good secateurs. I prefer the straight sided, long pointed variety, as they are easier to use in wreath making than those with curved blades. You may also find a pair of sharp florist's scissors handy, though not essential. Try to keep your secateurs and scissors clean and dry, for a rusty cutting tool will only frustrate you with its inefficiency. Rub a little kitchen oil over the blades when tools are not in use, or sewing machine oil is excellent if it's handy. Secateurs are good for cutting plant material of most thicknesses likely to be used in wreaths and garlands. Should a really thick pruning need to be severed, you may need to saw through it! You are, however, unlikely to be using much that is so heavy, as wreaths and garlands will not easily support heavy materials.

Wire cutters

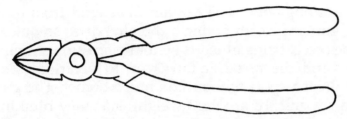

You may like to have a pair of wire cutters handy. The fine gauge florist's wire can easily be cut with secateurs, but this is not ideal. These wire cutters will make the job quick and simple, and will be necessary, anyway, should you be using heavy gauge wire. Never be tempted to cut any wire with your scissors for it will dent the blades and you will then have to re-sharpen them.

Glue gun

I can't imagine working with dried flowers, wreaths and garlands without my glue gun! These are fairly new innovations for dried floral work, but in the few years that they've been adapted to that purpose, glue guns have proved to be very useful. I believe these guns have long been used by carpet layers and plumbers for applying various glues and sealants. Little did they know that crafty people everywhere would become reliant upon these guns for something quite different! An electric glue gun is best described as being shaped like a hand gun, with or without a trigger, and having a cavity at the back into which a pellet of solid glue is pushed. In a gun without a trigger, the pellet is pushed through the gun by the user's thumb, or, with a trigger controlled gun, it is pulled through the gun by the trigger action. The pellet is melted at very high temperatures within the gun and emerges through the nozzle as liquid glue. This glue dries almost clear, and extremely quickly, and forms a strong bond. The wonderful benefits from using a glue gun are worth noting – the glue dries so quickly that the object being glued is held in place almost immediately, and the nozzle allows you to push glue into hard-to-reach spots without too much bother. The guns heat fairly quickly, are light weight, and they plug into any normal power socket. A warning, though, about the heat of the glue; do be careful to keep your fingers away from the hot liquid glue, as contact with it can be painful!

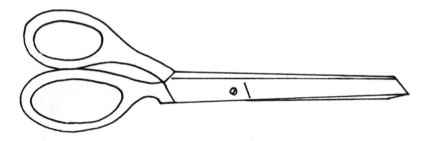

Scissors

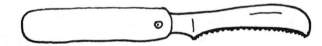

Pruning saw

Your workplace

For your own convenience, your work bench should be a dedicated spot. Easier written than done, I know. Don't try to keep all your work things on the kitchen table unless you plan to clean up after each session. Dried flowers, naturally, tend to drop bits all over the place while you work, and you can try with all your might to keep things tidy as you go, but I'll wager that you'll find it as difficult as I do! There is nothing wrong with working outside providing you have a power point for your glue gun. Or, perhaps, you could do most of your cutting and preparation of all your trimmings out of the house in the garden. It is much easier to sweep flower debris back into the garden than to extract it from the carpet! However, whatever your options may be for situating your work bench, try to have some permanent, dedicated area, if possible. You will welcome being able to down tools, leaving your work as is, ready to be resumed later, where you finished off.

Having somewhere to hang the wreath or garland as work progresses is also ideal. We tend to work on these while bending over from above – which is not as they will be viewed when complete. Hanging your work at intervals will give you an instant impression of its finished appearance. You will see unwanted colour blocking, gaps or overcrowding at a glance this way, and will be able to rectify these small problems before it's too late.

If you are fortunate enough to have additional storage space around your bench, use it to hold boxes into which you have sorted your collection of dried flowers, pods, shells, nuts and the like, into colours, types and size. This may seem luxurious, but having even the colours of flowers sorted can instantly show you the quantities you have of one colour or another, and make the planning of a design much simpler.

Further in the book I'll be discussing in detail the preservation of flowers, and the various ways you can do this for yourself. If you should decide to dry and preserve your own flowers, rather than purchase them, having the facilities for doing this around your bench is ideal. Air drying of flowers is the most common method, and these drying bunches look wonderful while they

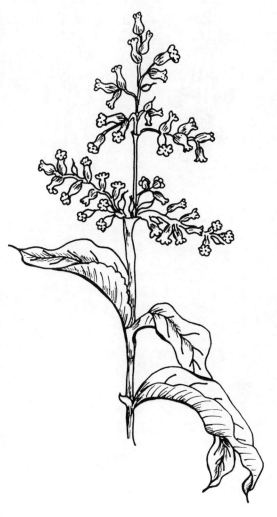

are hanging in groups to dry. All you need for this is an airy space up high where you can hang your bunches out of the way. You may need more bench space to hold various bottles of foliage being preserved in glycerine. These bottles should be able to stand well out of your way while working, and be left undisturbed for some weeks.

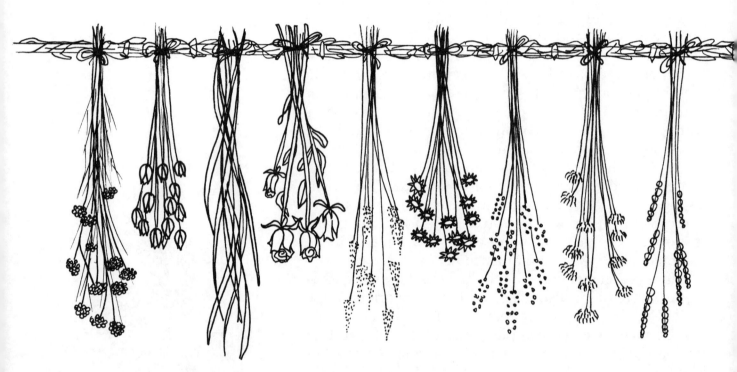

Floral bunches hanging in groups to dry

Themes, trimmings and bases

When, as a child, I asked yet another particularly diffi-cult question, a dear relative of mine would reply 'how long is a piece of string'! I had no idea what she meant at the time, but I do remember being certain she was telling me that there was no true answer to my ques-tion! This cryptic answer may well be applied to the question of 'just what do you use to decorate wreaths and garlands?'. The possibilities are truly endless, and the scope for personal expression unbounded.

As your enthusiasm grows for making floral decora-tions, you will automatically start seeing possibilities in everyday materials around you. It's impossible to make a definitive list for you – as I said above, the scope is amazing, but I can give you some ideas that will assist you in designing your wreaths and garlands.

Themes are important to consider when deciding on design, and they usually centre around a special occa-sion, the time of the year, seasons, or the personal taste of someone to whom you will present your wreath or garland. Weddings, birthdays and anniversaries, Christ-mas, Church harvest celebrations, a new house, Easter, and a redecorated room are all going to prompt you to design a wreath or garland in a certain way. Dried flow-ers – though sometimes fresh will be more appropriate – are usually going to play a large part in the design, so consider these along with colour, texture and size.

Consider gathering up the more unusual (compared to flowers) things in nature. Driftwood and shells will combine to make a beach house wreath; wood shavings and pretty bark will make a 'woodsy' wreath when com-bined with bundles of potpourri; dried herbs and bun-dles of spices combine to make a kitchen wreath; and

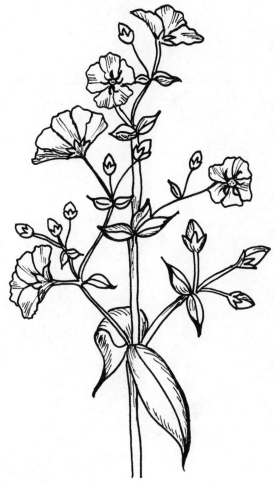

painted eggs, straw and yellow flowers would make a fabulous Easter wreath. Garlands may be purely floral, or they may be made up of the same materials suggested for wreaths. Perhaps they could be covered in small pumpkins, corn, garlic, onions and the like for a harvest celebration, or wrapped in superb variegated foliage that is either preserved or fresh. Later in the book I discuss the most successful ways of drying and preserving your own flowers and foliage.

There are numerous man-made materials or objects that look wonderful in wreaths and garlands. Ribbons and braids of all colours and textures, small wrapped and ribbon–tied parcels, Christmas baubles, painted wooden cut–outs, wrapped sweets, small new or old toys and artificial flowers are only a few suggestions. You may like to gather these objects as you find them available, but it is more likely that you will only know exactly what trimmings you need to gather when you design your garland or wreath.

Making your own wreath bases

Most craft and floristry outlets now have a good range of ready–made wreath bases for sale. These come in a variety of sizes and types, most of which are made in Asia, and are consequently inexpensive. I have no aversion to using a ready-made base, in fact I frequently do, but I also enjoy making my own bases when the materials are to hand. The materials able to be used in wreath bases are surprisingly varied. Most vines, straw, raffia, willow, bamboo, bracken fern and reed leaves are suitable, given that there are optimum times of their growth when they are best harvested for wreath bases.

Vine bases

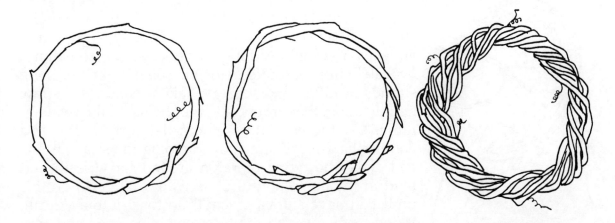

Three stages of making a vine wreath base

Ornamental grapevines provide excellent wreath material. It is best to cut long prunings from your vine during autumn, when it is crusty with attractive bark and tendrils, and there is still enough sap in the vine to allow flexibility. If vines are too brittle they will not bend into shape; rather they will snap or bend at unattractive angles.

Take a length of vine and twist it into the approximate size of the circle you need. Overlap and twist the ends around each other. Take another length of vine and twist it over and over around the circle, until it is all used. Repeat this process until your wreath base is thick enough. Try to start and finish vine lengths at different spots, if possible. Do not cut off the tendrils, or even the dried leaves. The tendrils will look attractive and the leaves will fall off anyway. I like to make as many wreath bases, in different sizes, as my collection of vine prunings will allow then leave them flat in a warm, dry spot to await use. They will eventually become quite rigid and set in their shape.

Straw bases

Tying a straw or raffia wreath base together

This is a slightly messy material to use, but its bright, sunny yellow colour is worth the effort. It's quite fun, anyway! You will need a quantity of straw (sometimes available from produce stores), some twine or long strands of raffia, and scissors. Take a handful of straw and tie it together around the middle using the twine or raffia. Lay the tied straw onto a flat surface, and add another handful of straw, overlapping the straw at one end. Take the twine or raffia around the wreath and bind in the new handful of straw. Continue to do this until you have sufficient length to twist into a wreath. When ready, overlap the two remaining ends and continue binding the straw, adding several more lengths of twine or raffia to make it quite secure. You may have to push or pull it into a correct circular shape. To neaten your wreath, use your scissors to trim away all the odd bits of straw that protrude beyond the profile of your wreath. Store straw wreaths flat in a warm, dry place.

Bamboo bases

Only the fine twigs of bamboo are really suitable for wreath bases. The thicker strands are far too rigid to bend into a circle. Harvest fine bamboo twigs while they are green – and don't bother to remove the leaves. You should use the same principles to start making bamboo bases as you do with vine wreaths, twisting strands around the original circle of bamboo. As you may find it difficult to find sufficient long strands of bamboo, you may have to use many shorter lengths, and this will mean having to bind the strands together with raffia or twine. For details, follow the directions for making straw bases.

Bracken fern bases

I'm told that this was the basic material used by florists many years ago to make wreath and other floral bases. There is certainly a plentiful supply of bracken (some would say to pest proportions), but do be sure not to take bracken, or any other plant, from a National Park or other protected area.

Bracken grows on a long, flexible stem. The very old stems are less suitable than those stems of medium height, as they are too rigid, though the foliage of these older stems can be incorporated into the base. Quantities needed vary according to the size of the base, but the very nature of bracken foliage – coarse, fairly stiff and bulky – will make it more suited to larger wreaths than small.

Work with fresh bracken as you would with straw, using twine or raffia to bind the bracken fronds into a rope. You will find that you need three or four leaves and stems in each bundle that you overlap with the previous lot. You can always come back and add more layers to your wreath base if it is not thick enough. Cut away the thick part of the stem and rather than crush the fronds, wrap them around the bundle and bind to secure. When you overlap the ends of the wreath you may like to wrap this overlap area to make it smoother. Bracken bases are fairly good for fresh flower wreaths, as the fronds hold some water and the base and flowers can be misted with water to keep everything fresh. If using bracken as a base for dried trimmings, make and leave the wreath until it has dried thoroughly. You will find hot glue will not adhere well to green surfaces. Bracken wreaths dry quickly, so leave them flat in a warm, dry area until ready.

Willow bases

Willow is a wonderfully flexible wood, and the long strands falling from the main branches are excellent wreath material. In Asia, these fine willow strands are dried in the sun, then the bark is pulled away to reveal the lovely white wood underneath. A time consuming project but the method produces very effective results. I have never been patient enough to do that for a wreath base – even a small one! I would best describe it as therapeutic, and think that willow fronds are, and always will be, beautiful in their natural state!

Take a handful of strands and tie them together at one end with twine or raffia. Bind these together, introducing more strands when the others thin out. Continue binding until you have a long rope, sufficient for the circumference of your wreath. Overlap these ends and continue to bind to secure. You can add more strands to build up thickness by laying them along the wreath and binding them in. Willow bases need to dry out before use, so store these flat in a warm, dry area until ready.

Don't overlook using pussy willow strands, too. This most attractive tree provides us with those soft catkins each spring, and if cut early in the season, these soft little buds will dry on the fronds and add an interesting texture to your wreath base. The willow known as 'tortured' willow is also an effective base material.

Reed bases

Reed leaves are best harvested while fresh and green, then hung upside down to air dry until you are ready to use them. It is possible to work with them green, but there is a lot of shrinkage with reed leaves and your bindings may have to be reworked to tighten things up. Reeds should be worked in the same way as willow. You are able to use a base made from dried reeds immediately.

Raffia bases

This fibre is harvested from the raffia palm, grown on the island of Madagascar, off the east coast of Africa. Similar raffia straw is also produced in some parts of Asia, mainly the Philippines. The fronds are harvested annually and no harm is done to the palm in the process. The narrow, straw-like fibres are very strong, and come in varied lengths, some quite long. Treat this fibre as you would willow strands, but take more care to bind the fibres very tightly. A raffia base needs to be bound very tightly, perhaps in a crisscross pattern, to keep it firm, as it tends to droop if not well secured. You may like to make a raffia base that can be exposed, rather than covered with trimmings. I suggest you make a very thick, tightly wrapped, four strand plait – the thickness of your proposed wreath base – and try to curve it, by pulling on the inside strand as you plait. This should then be easier to bind into a circle; overlap the ends and bind them. The overlap area will need to be disguised by some trimmings.

Drying and preserving flowers

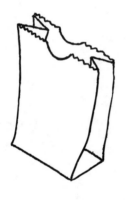

You can place nuts and pods into a paperbag to dry

There are plenty of pretty blooms, just right for floral work, that can easily be grown in your garden, and then dried in your home. There are two main ways of drying flowers – air drying and drying with dessicants. Depending on the type of flower or foliage you choose, it can be dried hanging upside down, standing in a suitable container, or simply lying in an airy box or bag.

The ideal room for drying plants, whatever the method, should be dark and airy, with good ventilation, and humidity free. Humidity will only promote the growth of fungus which will rot plant material, and render it useless. Too much light will fade the flowers very quickly. Ventilation is important, for it is the constant flow of dry air that removes moisture from the flowers.

When to harvest for air drying

The best time to pick flowers for drying is around midday, when the plant is likely to be relatively dry and any dew will have evaporated. Try to pick flowers just before they reach their prime. Seek out buds just about to open, rather than a full-blown flower. The tightness of a bud will give you more success in drying, than will a full flower on its way to shedding petals.

14

How to hang flowers to dry

This is the most common, and successful, method of air drying plants. Before you form the material into bunches prior to hanging, remove all the lower leaves and dry the stems with a towel. Group the flowers into bunches – around five or six stems – and tie them together with string or raffia. I prefer to use raffia, and I don't like using elastic bands. They seem too strong and can dent, or weaken, stems. Aim to have as little contact between the flowers as possible; fan them out and stagger the height of each flower if necessary.

Tie the bunch to a rod or rafter in the drying area. Arrange the bunches so that they do not touch while they are suspended, and be mindful of the amount of space allowed around the bunch, as air circulation is very important. It is better to dry a few well arranged bunches at one time, than to have many bunches close together, quietly and disastrously rotting away.

You will find that different plants take varied lengths of time to dry completely. This depends on the moisture content of the stems, rather than the petals. Flowers taken from their hanging position before they are completely dry soon wilt and flop, as their stems are still moist. You will eventually be experienced enough to plan ahead and have dried material ready for use anytime!

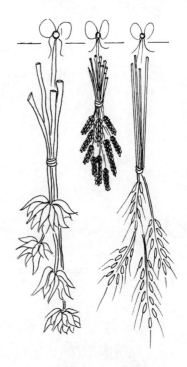

Floral bunches air drying

Air drying plants upright

There are a few common plants which need to be dried upright – hydrangeas, delphiniums or larkspurs and gypsophila are the most known. Stand them in a supportive container with only a little water in the bottom. As the water is absorbed the air drying takes over, and as the last of the water disappears your plant is well on the way to being dry.

Most of the cereal crop grains – wheat, oats and barley for example, can simply be stood in a tall container and allowed to dry. You can even use these green and allow them to dry in the arrangement.

Flat drying

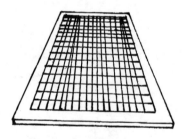

Insert flower stems through the wire mesh and leave to dry

There are a number of plants which can be simply laid in a box to dry. Foliage is an obvious choice here, and so are nuts, corn, fir cones and most seed pods. If you have something with a very short stem that needs to be dried upright, cover a box opening with wire netting and staple or tack it at the sides to secure. Insert the plant stem into the wire up to the flower head; the wire provides support. The air still circulates around the plant and it dries undistorted.

Drying plants using desiccants

There are few plants not able to be dried using desiccants. Desiccants draw out the moisture from the flower, leaving a dried, papery flower that is comparatively undistorted by the process. There are several suitable drying agents, borax, alum, fine sand and silica gel being the most common. The main advantage of this drying method is that your results are close to resembling the fresh flower – colour and shape are maintained. However, the main disadvantages are that desiccants can be expensive, and the method is somewhat testing of your patience! I have found through experience that desiccant drying is really only practical on a small scale, and that I tend to use it mainly for foliage, rather than for flowers. It is possible to layer many leaves into one container of desiccant, and I especially like the results gained with rose leaves. You would be surrounded by stacks of boxes containing drying flowers if you used this method on a large scale. Apart from the space needed, the financial investment in the large quantity of desiccant needed would deter many. This is not to say 'don't use it', but do bear these drawbacks in mind when gathering your materials for wreaths and garlands.

Using silica gel and borax

Silica gel looks like small sugar crystals. When it is dry the crystals are bright blue, turning to pink when moisture is absorbed. Silica gel can be re-used, by drying it out in the oven on a baking tray. This extracts the moisture. The crystals should be allowed to cool in the oven, then store in an airtight container until you wish to use them again.

Some experts suggest mixing borax with fine clean freshwater sand, and this idea has merit. Borax tends to go lumpy during use, and the fine grains of sand would prevent this. Borax is a common cleaning agent, and looks like granular flour.

It is not expensive, but can be fiddly to brush away from the flowers after the drying process is finished. Either way, with or without sand, borax is an efficient desiccant.

Seal a plastic food storer with its clip-on lid to keep the desiccant dry

Preparing flowers for drying desiccants

Cut your flowers when they are in their prime, and as dry as possible. Remove any stems, and avoid blemished leaves or petals. I like to dry leaves with desiccants as they hold their colour well. Search for pretty leaves as well as flowers, and remember that there are no hard and fast rules about results from using desiccants – every flower is a gamble! As the stems of flowers dried in this way are cut off, you should plan on using these as flowers to be wired or glued closely to your wreath or garland.

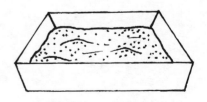

Cover an open tray of desiccant with a heavy layer of newspapers

How to use the desiccant

Fill an airtight box, cake tin or something similar with a layer of dessicant about 2 cm (1") thick. Place the blooms onto this layer, being sure they don't have their petals touching and that the bases of the flowers are well supported. Slowly pour the desiccant around the blooms, using a small paint brush to push the grains into the petals and completely surround the flower. This is important, for any area of the bloom not in contact with the desiccant will not dry out properly. Once the blooms are surrounded and covered, add more desiccant to seal the blooms completely and replace the lid on the container. Seal the edges with tape to be sure it's airtight.

Desiccants dry flowers very quickly, and you should check on progress after about two days. Flowers that spend excess time in desiccants become too brittle and often simply disintegrate! If you are using silica gel, the crystals will be deep pink when they have absorbed the moisture. You will have to brush aside borax to test the tops of petals for dryness. If you are satisfied that the flowers are dry, gently brush away the desiccant and lift the flower, placing it on a dry, flat surface. Using a small paint brush remove any remaining borax or silica gel crystals from within the flowers. Use the flowers immediately, or store them, separated by tissue paper, in an airtight container until needed.

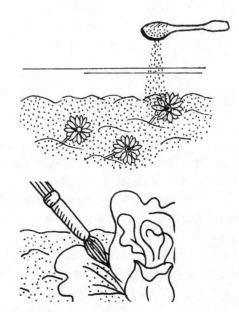

Spooning desiccant over flowers to be dried

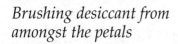

Brushing desiccant from amongst the petals

Preserving foliage using glycerine

The process of preserving foliage differs from drying plant material, as instead of removing the moisture content, this process replaces moisture with a glycerine solution that preserves and stabilises the plant, rather than drying it. Glycerine preservation will only succeed with mature foliage, not new growth. Hard-stemmed plants such as camellias, copper beech and eucalyptus varieties need to have their stems cut at an extreme angle to allow for maximum absorption of glycerine, while other stems, such as ferns, should be crushed to allow this process to occur. Set aside some tall, stable, narrow-necked containers to hold the foliage.

Mix a solution of half boiling water, half glycerine and stir, or shake, the mixture thoroughly. Pour about 8 to 10 cm (3" to 4") of the glycerine solution into each

Foliage stems in a bottle of glycerine solution

container, and insert the stems of foliage. Leave the containers in a dark, cool spot for about a week. As soon as you notice small beads of glycerine forming on the underside or tips of leaves at the top of the branch the process is complete. Remove the preserved foliage immediately and either wash the branch in warm water and detergent, or wipe it free of glycerine with paper towel. Plant material left too long in glycerine can ultimately rot, as it retains too much moisture.

Single leaves, such as large ivy leaves, can be soaked individually in a glycerine solution. This reaction will be quick, and you are able to see at a glance how the process is progressing. Take the leaf from the solution when finished, then wash and dry well. This is often a good way of experimenting on unfamiliar foliage, to see if larger branches are worth preserving.

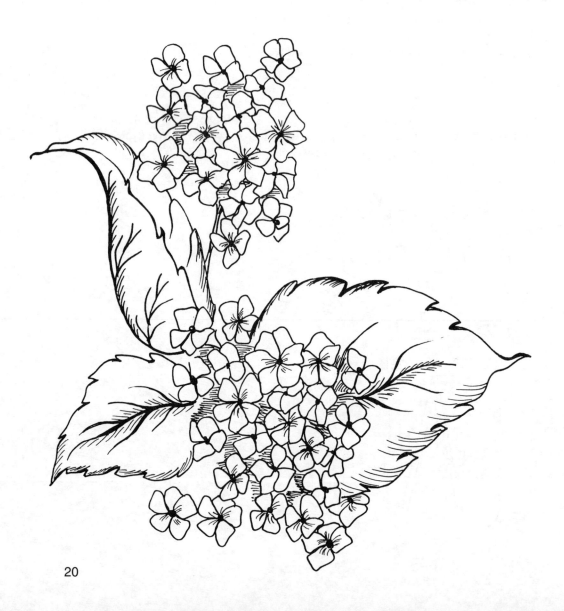

Colouring and storing flowers and foliage

Dyeing with glycerine

It is possible to add water soluble dyes to the glycerine solution, and I have had moderate success with this. The dyes give the plant a permanent colour, which can be a good thing, for glycerine preservation does tend to darken the foliage. Green and blue dyes are interesting on all foliage, especially on eucalyptus, and reds are interesting with camellia leaves. I generally don't like tinted plants, as I find them artificial and therefore at odds with the remainder of the decorations. However, some colours, especially green, can enhance rather than spoil, and this is all a matter of experimentation. The quantities of dye needed are another matter for experimentation, and you simply add the dye to the glycerine mixture once it has cooled.

Dyeing fresh flowers

Water soluble dyes can be added to the water in fresh flowers, too. This can mean leaving the flowers in only a small amount of water to dry as they absorb the last of the water, or allowing fresh young flowers to absorb as much of the dye in their normal drinking water as necessary to colour them, then air drying them.

Bleaching flowers and foliage

Bleach may also be added to a glycerine solution, and though this is a gamble, it is worth trying. Proportions of bleach should be equal to glycerine, and flowers should be left as for dyeing and preserving with glycerine. Interesting streaked effects can occur with bleaching, especially in aspidistra leaves. Flowers that are less spongy than others seem to react well to bleach.

Painting dried flowers and foliage

I enjoy painting dried pods and twigs, for they can become very useful bright spots of colour in any wreath or garland. This unnatural effect does not seem to bother me as much as some garishly tinted flowers. There is much to be said for painting with metallic paints, though this tends to be a visual signal for Christmas wreaths and garlands. You will have to be fairly selective about the colours you put with metallic paints to avoid them looking like Christmas decorations. A little metallic paint, say bronze or silver, can look good mixed with other trimmings, and gold paint seems to blend with just about anything, be it fresh or dried. Metallic paints will

Group flowers closely together before spray painting

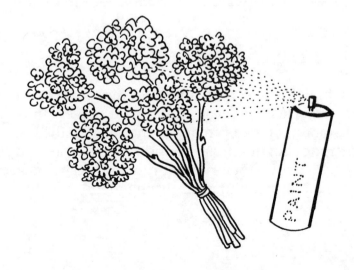

automatically make a wreath or garland take on a formal appearance, unless the objects mixed with it are shiny plastic or chrome, and then the overall appearance tends to be contemporary. In short, be cautious in your use of metallic paints when the wreath or garland is not for Christmas! When you do use them for Christmas trims, the effect is magical and most atmospheric.

Twigs, pods – such as poppy heads – and nuts look wonderful when painted, and virtually any colour will do. You can hand paint them using artists' acrylic paints from tubes or bottles, or use a spray pressure pack of oil paint. The oil paints will dry very glossy; the acrylic paints will have a matt finish.

Clear gloss paint sprayed onto natural items gives them a shiny, deepened colouring, and can sometimes be all you need to colour a wreath or garland trimmed with naturally dried twigs, leaves and pods.

It is possible to spray flowers with acrylic paint to re-colour them. This method is often used by florists to give flowers a hue closer to the colour scheme for which they have been requested. Some colours are totally against the natural colouring of the flower, and look simply awful – blue carnations, for example! However, this method has merit, if only to enhance the natural colour of the flower. Flowers, especially those air dried, will fade, and by spraying them with paint the colour is restored. Only some flowers are really suitable – sea

lavender, hydrangeas and some bunched roses for example – bunch the flowers tightly together, mask the leaves then spray lightly. Too much paint can tint the foliage and bases of flowers, spoiling the effect.

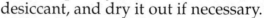

Storing flowers

You can easily be left with a surplus of dried flowers, and while it's possible to leave flowers air drying, dust and light will have their damaging effects. It's best to take the thoroughly dried bunches and wrap them in tissue paper, taking care to have the flower heads well protected. As you are using your flowers for wreaths and garlands, you will be able to trim away some length from stalks, giving you more storage space. Layer these wrapped bunches into large cardboard cartons, top-to-tail fashion with stems between other flower heads to make use of the space. Cover the carton and store the flowers until needed.

While glycerine dried flowers should be stored in the same way, do not ever mix them with air dried flowers in the same storage box. Retained moisture in glycerine dried flowers will ultimately travel to the air dried flowers and rot will set in. Wrap glycerine foliage exactly as for air dried flowers and store separately.

Place some borax or silica gel in small bags in amongst the flowers to absorb any moisture remaining. Check on them frequently to see what moisture is absorbed by the desiccant, and dry it out if necessary.

Making a wreath

Depending on the type of base you're using, there are several methods to choose from when fastening trimmings to make a wreath.

Using a glue gun

This glue works best with natural trimmings and some found objects. Just a small mound of glue is sufficient to hold most stems or flowers. I find that it's easier to place the glue onto the wreath or garland, then push the stem into the glue, rather than gluing the stem prior to positioning it. The hot glue from the gun dries very quickly, so you should have decided the positions of your trimmings before applying the glue. It will not fasten green fruit or vegetables in place, but is ideal for pine cones, twigs, dried flowers and pods, grasses, fabric flowers and matt-surfaced found objects. Shiny painted surfaces are usually successful, though the paint may prevent a heavy object being securely connected by hot glue. If something is to be painted, I usually glue it in place first, then apply the paint. This is my favourite way of making wreaths and garlands quickly, and I tend to use it more than wiring. It is possible to use the two methods together in one wreath, and in fact, it is sensible to do so when combining objects or materials of differing weights.

25

Wiring a wreath

Wiring fir cones for use in wreaths

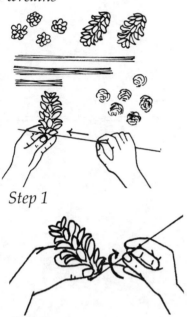

Step 1

Step 2

This method is time-honoured and, when properly, the most secure. You will have to bundle your objects into groups, or singly if appropriate, and wind around them the end of a length of medium-gauge florist's wire. You should leave a tail of wire that will fasten onto the wreath. Be sure that the wire is very tightly wound off after wrapping it around your bundles – wire is springy, and will take any chance it gets to unwind! Use a pair of pointed wire pliers, twist the ends of the wire into rope-like coils and then bend the coils down into the wreath. This wiring method is the slowest, but by far the most satisfactory when heavy objects are involved. If there is not an obvious long stem around which to fasten wire, such as in pine-cones, drill a hole though the base or the stem and thread the wire through this. Remember, as mentioned earlier when discussing glue guns, that, where needed, wiring and gluing can be combined to make your wreaths and garlands.

Wiring bunches of flowers for use in wreaths

Step 1

Step 2

A wound garland of French lavender   *Silk roses*

Gingham ribbon wreath   *Cottage garden wreath*

Festive berries and silk roses

Romantic roses

Sparkles for Christmas

Beachcomber's holiday

Autumn pickings

Wheat with plaited raffia

Flowers with sphagnum moss

A bouquet swag

A small dried flower swag

Waxed fruit with flowers in a vertical swag

Winding with twine or wire

This is probably the simplest way to decorate a wreath or garland. There are no glues to work with, and, providing the winding is very secure, the wreath or garland will last well. It is also a good method for working with fresh flowers, or seasonal decorations that are temporary. Gather your wreath making materials, your base and bunches or groups of flowers, and have a supply of fine, strong fuse wire that is wound onto a reel, or a ball of twine. Fine wire is available in various gauges from electrical stores, as it is used in bulk by electricians. It is not expensive and is most efficient.

Wire for winding wreaths and garlands

You need to plan the sequence of trimmings on your wreath well, for as you are working with a continuous piece of wire or twine, it will be very difficult for you to unwind it and return to some spot that is not decorated to your liking. Apart from the frustration, the trimmings will all fall off! Be sure that there is a hanging hook installed in some part of the wreath, and that you have planned where your garland needs to have hooks.

Wind your wire or twine around the wreath and tie it off, leaving the long, continuous piece in place. Place your first bunch of flowers over the wire and wind the wire around the bunch, securing it. Be sure to add bunches at the sides of the wreath. As soon as you have secured a bunch, place the next bunch down, and continue to wind. Wiring directions are instinctive, with right handed people winding in an anti-clockwise direction, and left handed people winding clockwise. Continue to wind and secure bunches of flowers until your wreath is nearly covered. As you approach the starting point, gently lift the first bunch placed and tuck the stems of the last bunch underneath the flower heads, wiring carefully, and being sure to tie your twine or wire off securely.

Winding a wreath with wire. Note that the hanging hook is in place

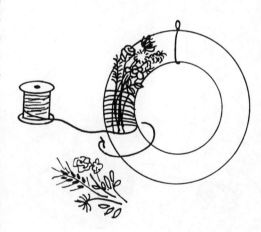

Try to decorate these wreaths or garlands generously, as the winding material will show through on those sparsely covered.

A wreath to wear

A circlet for the bride

One of the prettiest headpiece fashions to emerge for brides and their attendants in recent years is the floral wreath or circlet. A bridesmaid or flower girl can wear one trimmed to complement the colour of her gown, and the bride's garland can be made from quite different flowers, while still giving the wedding party a co-ordinated look, due to the shape of their headpieces. Floral circlets are an ideal solution for less formal celebrations, as they can work well without a tulle veil attached, and are a delightful choice for second marriages.

These wreaths or circlets differ from decorative wreaths in that they have a soft, flexible base. We don't want brides to have sore heads from carrying around a solid ring of vine prunings! This soft, flexible base is made from twisted pipe cleaners, and is fitted to the exact head size of the wearer, so comfort is assured.

To make the base

Gather up some of the thicker, longer pipe cleaners that can be used for craft projects. They are sometimes known as 'chenille' pipe cleaners. It doesn't really matter what colour they are, as they will be covered with ribbon. Don't despair if they are not available to you, as the common pipe cleaner is quite adequate, the only difference being that you will have to join more together to create the length and thickness desired for the base.

Start by twisting two or more together to create a strip long enough to equal the distance around the wearer's head. Circlets usually look good sitting just on the forehead and just above the ears. If they are too small and sit on top of the head they tend to slide off, or need dozens of hair-pins to keep them attached. The last thing needed by a small flower girl is her pretty circlet sliding off her shiny hair! When the ideal spot for the circlet to rest is decided upon, twist the ends of the pipe cleaners together so that they are secure. Continue to wind more lengths of cleaners around this original circle until your band of pipe cleaners is about 1.5cm (5/8") thick.

Choose some satin ribbon that is the colour of the bridesmaid's dress, or something that will tone with the flowers used on the circlet. Pin the end of this ribbon to the circlet, angling it so that it will wind around the circlet easily, and start to wind, continuing until all pipe cleaners are covered. Hand stitch, or glue, the ribbon ends to secure them. What you have now is a smooth, comfortable, flexible ring as your circlet base.

What flowers to use

If your wedding is in winter, you may well need to consider using silk or dried flowers, or perhaps a combination of both. This means several things. You will not have the dilemma of keeping fresh flowers from wilting, the flowers can be decided upon with confidence well in advance and, therefore, are not subject to the vagaries of the weather. Also, the bride and her maids can keep their circlets as a lovely memento of the wedding day. Fresh flowers are always charming and, if they are readily available, totally suitable for this purpose. You will have to allocate time close to the ceremony to make them, though you will be able to make the bases well in advance. Once fresh flower circlets are made, keep them moist and in the refrigerator until it's time to wear them.

The size of the flowers you choose is fairly important. Very large flowers, such as lillies, would look entirely out of proportion if mixed with smaller flowers, and used exclusively would make the circlet look too big. You will need to tie smaller flowers, such as violets, into small bunches before you can wind them into your circlet. Do consider the softening effect of adding small sprays of gypsophila, as these tiny flowers blend with most others and create a cloud-like halo around your circlet. In fact, circlets made only from this flower look very pretty indeed, and are delightful for all-white or cream weddings. You may like to add long ribbons to trail down from the centre back of the circlet.

Making your own fabric flowers

You may like to consider making your own fabric flowers to fasten to the base. Refer to the instructions for

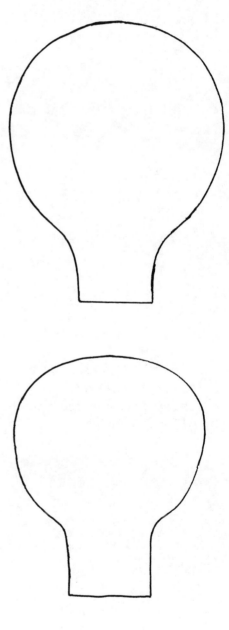

a. Petal shapes for bride's floral circlet

29

making the bride's garland from stiffened fabric flowers on page 46. This was achieved by using a product called fabric stiffener. I suggest you make your own flowers from fabrics such as organza or stiff voile, or similar fabrics. First, coat the entire piece of fabric with fabric stiffener and peg it on the clothes line to allow it to dry. Then cut out petals, using the petal pattern provided. I suggest you cut 12 large petals, and 7 smaller petals for each flower, though you should experiment with this. Cut a strip of unstiffened fabric on the bias (diagonally across the fabric) about 2 cm (1") wide, and cut it again into 5 cm (2") lengths. Moisten each small piece with fabric stiffener, then twist them as if to make a spiral rope. The stiffener will hold them in this shape, and, when they're dry, you should trim the ends diagonally to neaten. These small spirals become the stamens of the flowers, and you will need about 4-5 for each flower. Bundle together the dried stamens, and overlap the smaller petals around these, then overlap the larger petals around these. Using a strong sewing needle and thread, stitch through and then wind thread, around the 'stem' of the flower to secure the petals in place.

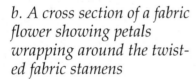

b. A cross section of a fabric flower showing petals wrapping around the twisted fabric stamens

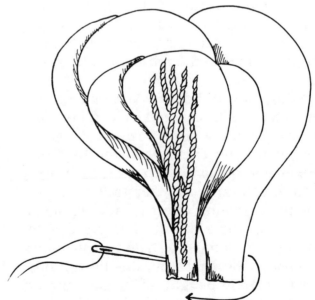

Winding flowers onto the circlet

Gather up the flowers you anticipate using. If fresh, such as stemmed rose-buds, remove thorns and foliage from the stem, shortening the stems to a uniform length, say about 10 cm (4") long. Using the technique described earlier in the book for winding a wreath, start to wind flowers onto the base, using narrow ribbon or embroidery floss that is the same colour as the ribbon that is covering the pipe cleaners. Be sure to cover the sides of the base, keeping the inner edge free from flowers, as this rests against the head of the wearer. If you find winding fabric flowers awkward because the stems are too long and stiff, consider shortening the stem (below the threads that are securing the petals together) and stitching, or gluing with hot glue, the flowers to the base.

a. Flowers already wound into place
b. Flower stems being wound with narrow ribbon to secure
c. Ribbon wound around to hide pipe cleaners
d. The ends of pipe cleaners twisted together to secure

Attaching a tulle veil to the bride's circlet

This can be done in two ways, depending on the bride's preferences. As tulle is very wide, it is possible to centre the tulle over the bride's head, so that some of it falls to below her shoulders – or further – as a face veil, and the remainder falls down the back to whatever length is desired. Simply place the circlet down over the tulle to hold it in position, removing the tulle after the ceremony and replacing the circlet.

The other way is to gather the end of the tulle and bind it into a narrow band. Stitch this band at the back of the circlet, so that it falls from under the flowers, or, if you wish, so that it falls from within the circlet. Apply flowers around the circlet, stopping them either side of where the veil flows out of the circlet. If the veil does emerge from within the circlet, it will have to remain attached throughout the wearing of the circlet. A veil that emerges from under the circlet can be attached temporarily and removed during the celebrations.

Garlands

These delightful streamers are one of the most impressive floral decorations I know. They take as much time to make, proportionately, as a wreath, and they are as enduring. Their only drawback, if there is one at all, is the need to install some form of secure hanging device and this can be difficult if you wish to hang your garland against a wall. As each garland will have its own unique position and possible logistical dilemma, I propose only to tell you of how to make them and install them, and give you many suggestions for trimmings and possible locations.

Winding a garland onto a rope base

What is a garland?

Sometimes known as swags, these decorated ropes or streamers are looped between and over objects, often symmetrically, to add decoration to a room. They can be extremely effective in providing instant decorating impact, and they can be as grand or simple as you wish them to be. I always feel garlands look wonderful; they are exciting visually, and when they are eventually removed leave what appears a very dull space indeed!

Where to decorate with garlands

Symmetry and balance is important in the effect of garlands. You should look for decorative opportunities where symmetry is possible, such as, for example, the mantelpiece, where, perhaps, one or two loops could travel across the front of the mantel, with tails falling from either side. Smaller garlands can be draped across bedheads or steads, and even lighter ones could rest across the top of a painting. Consider draping, or winding, a long garland down a staircase rail, with a large grouping of more trimming around each stair post at the base of the stairs. Other suggested locations include the top

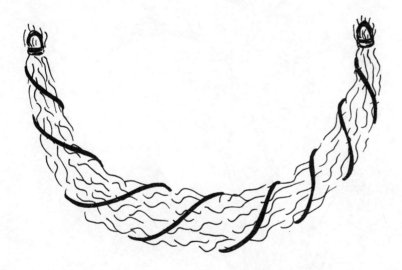

of the kitchen dresser, door and window frames, entrance ways, church altar rails, mirrors, exposed beams, window seats, and around the edge of tables – especially those holding a wedding or birthday cake. You need to give serious consideration to how the garland is to be supported, as decorations crumbling to the floor are to be avoided! Install hooks used for hanging pictures, fine nylon lines attached to fish hooks (take great care with

A wound single garland base using bamboo, straw, bracken or raffia. Extend these into as many loops as you require

the points) or butcher's hooks – they are all suitable, depending on your particular situation. If no hooks can be installed, consider tying the garland into place, or, at the last resort, simply using gravity to balance it into place while it is draped over something. This last suggestion is risky, but very possible if the garland is well out of the way of enquiring hands.

If you are using fresh flowers or produce, consider whether you will be able to mist the garland with water. Also consider the light, air flow and any direct sunlight that may adversely affect a fresh flower garland.

Bases for garlands

Traditional bases were rope, or plaited raffia. These were simply measured by looping or draping the rope over the distance to be decorated and cutting off the rope at the required spot, and this method still holds good today. Other materials for bases can be used. Plastic bin liners can be split down each side and opened up, then crushed and bound into a rope, and cut to the desired length. They are light and easy to manipulate and very inexpensive, but, they can only be wired or wound with twine; don't use hot glue on a plastic bin liner! For heavier garlands, chicken wire rolled around sphagnum moss is ideal, as the wire can be bent into shape and the moss can hold quite a lot of moisture which will benefit fresh flowers. For very small, permanent garlands cut a circular wreath right through on one side, and on the opposite side, cut a V two-thirds through from the outside edge. Open out the wreath, folding it down into two half-circles at the V point. You now have two symmetrical half-circles ready for decoration. You will have to install hanging hooks at each end and in the centre, and allow for some material, such as raffia, to fall from each end and the centre, if needed for tails. Wreaths made from straw, bamboo, twigs and reeds will be pliable enough to shape as suggested. Vine and willow wreaths may be a little tough and rigid to cut in this way.

When considering bases, the important point is how long you wish your garland to be in place. If working with dried flowers and you plan a decorative garland for all year round, you will need to be especially careful to fix the trimmings and fasten the garland securely, but moisture retention in your base is not a consideration. If the garland is a seasonal one, such as for Christmas, and you decorate the same area year after year, you may wish to make a basic rope base that can have trimmings removed and can then be stored for next year. Weddings will probably involve fresh flowers, so temporary bases can be good here. If you work with flowers often, and frequently are called upon to decorate the same church, you may like to fashion wire bases that can be tied into place and re-used often. If your foray

Winding a garland onto crushed bin liners

into garland making is likely to be once only, a bin-liner base may be just right for you, as the whole thing can be detached and disposed of at the end of the day.

Attaching trimmings to garlands

The various techniques used in decorating wreaths apply to garlands. You will find the easiest way to hold trimmings is by winding, using fine wire or twine. If using chicken wire you will tuck the stems of single flowers or wired bunches into the spaces in the wire, then fasten them with more wire or twine. Bin liner bases will first be crushed and wound with twine or wire, then the trimmings should be wired on. Do not use a hot melt glue gun to hold trimmings to plastic. Natural sisal rope or plaited raffia can be glued or wound, but only use glue for dried flowers.

You will find that most heavy trimmings need to be wired to be really secure. Heavy gauge florist's wire is most suitable and can be bought in bulk from florist's supply shops. Hard objects, such as nuts, need to be drilled and wired as for wreaths, and fresh fruit can be wired by pushing two wires through about 2 cm (1") below the stem in a cross shape, then twisting the ends of the wire together to make a single strand. One wire in a heavy piece of fruit will not give you the control you need. Bear in mind that fruit, such as apples and citrus

Fresh fruit wired for garland making. Select only firm, or slightly under ripe fruit or vegetables

fruit, will not last much longer than 7 to 10 days in a garland. Bunches of fresh flowers will be temporary, and may be wired or wound, whichever seems appropriate.

If working on a raffia base, extra strands of raffia may be used to tie or wind the trimmings in place.

Trimmings to use in garlands

Virtually anything used on a wreath can be used as trimming on a garland. Dried and fresh flowers, fruit, nuts, shells, small wrapped presents, bags of potpourri, ribbon tied in bows, and wrapped sweets are just some suggestions. As I mentioned above, the method of fixing them to your garland will depend on the type of base you choose, the length of time you plan it to be in place and the weight of the material you are fixing in place. Do be very conscious of weight in a garland, and the type of support you give it – remember – no crumbling, falling garlands! The trimmings on a garland can be heavy enough to distort the shape of the curved sections. Try not to allow heavy trimmings to sit in the centre of these curved pieces; aim to have them on the top sections, where very often they are supported by a mantelpiece, or similar.

Flowers and foliage

Some flowers suitable for air-drying

larkspurs
roses, especially buds
wheat and other grains
pyrethrum daisies
lavender of all sorts
marigolds, expecially African
achillea
poppy seed heads
helichrysum daisies
hops
sea lavender
santolina
daffodils
gypsophila
freesias
eucalypt leaves
ranunculas
peonie buds
jonquils
lilac
delphiniums
zinnias
lupins
buddleia
asters
celosia or cockscomb
proteas
echinops
eryngium orsea holly
flowers suitable for dessicant drying

Flowers suitable for desiccant drying

daisies of all varieties
roses
rose leaves
pittostrium leaves
hydrangeas
carnations
chrysanthemums
marigolds
ferns, especially maidenhair
some herb flowers, especially garlic
hyacinths
sweet peas
peonies
echinops
vibernum of most varieties
lilly of the valley
agapanthus florets
honeysuckle
lilac
anemones
lupins
snow drops
gerberas
santolina
rose hips
blossom buds
asters
zinnias
cornflowers

Foliage suitable for preserving with glycerine

camellias
aspidistras
holly
pussy willow stems
tortured willow stems
traditional willow stems
citrus leaves
ivy of all varieties
eleagnus
eucalyptus
ornamental figs
ornamental flax
small palm leaves
strelitzia
iris
beech leaves
molucella
fatsia
papyrus
some bamboos

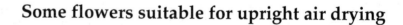

Some flowers suitable for upright air drying

hydrangeas
wheat and other grains
most grasses
statice
sea lavender
gypsophila
some eucalypt leaves
proteas
pussy willow
tortured willow
traditional willow
bullrushes

Projects shown on colour pages

Page 1

A wound garland of French lavender

Here you can see the effectiveness of choosing one flower only. Traditional lavender is wound onto the painted vine base using medium gauge wire. Wire the lavender into small bunches first and be sure to place bunches so that the sides of the base are well covered. The bow is tied first, then glued into place with hot glue. The woven fibre in the ribbon is known as 'sinimay' ribbon. It is made from fine coconut fibres and comes from the Philippines. I've simply painted it in a soft lavender to match the flowers and base, and allowed it to dry before gluing it into place. The moth-repellent qualities of lavender are renowned, and I like to hang wreaths like this one inside the door of my linen cupboard, or in walk-in cupboards. Every so often I wipe over the back of the wreath base with lavender oil to refresh the scent of the flowers.

Silk roses

These have been fixed with a hot glue gun to the heart-shaped vine base. The roses are first detached from their stems and are glued close together on the wreath base, silk leaves mingling with the flowers. I find that some silk flowers are too brightly coloured for my liking, and I overcome this by lightly spraying the finished wreath – sometimes minus the leaves – with gold paint. This softens the brightness of the flowers and gives glowing, 'antiqued' flowers that have a lovely old-world feel.

Gingham ribbon wreath

This is one of the simplest wreaths to decorate. Start winding a length of ribbon around the heart base by fixing one ribbon end just to one side of the top point of the heart. Fix it into position at the back of the wreath with hot glue, angling it so that the ribbon will wind smoothly around the wreath. Continue winding firmly until the ribbons overlap at the starting point, then cut and glue the end. Tuck flowers under the ribbon, as shown, adding a little glue if desired. Tie a ribbon bow and glue it to the top of the heart. This idea works well for Christmas wreaths, too. Wind tartan ribbon around your wreath base and tuck in fresh holly, berries or pine leaves.

Cottage garden wreath

A vine base has had dried flowers in glowing colours glued all over it. The flowers are fixed in position with hot melt glue, in single stems, not in bunches. Any combination of dried flowers would be successful, though you should try to combine flowers of differing sizes and textures. Give some consideration to colour combinations, as colour plays an important design role in floral wreaths. Often you can pull together the colour scheme of a difficult, or badly furnished, room by harmonising flowers with the room's colours – thus making the furnishings in the room look a little more deliberate. The flowers are glued to face a certain direction around the wreath, and the stems of the previously glued flowers are overlapped with the blossoms of the next. The shorter stemmed daisies have some of their stems removed and then are glued flat, or facing straight upwards.

Page 2

Festive berries and silk roses

A vine base has been covered with painted waxed fruit and berries, and small silk roses. The berries and roses have been lightly sprayed with gold paint, still allowing their bright colours to show through in places. The silk roses are detached from their stems before gluing. The bow is made of gold-painted crushed paper ribbon. It is widely available at craft shops, and comes in a coil that requires some patience in opening and flattening. Tie the bow first, leaving long tails, then paint it, or spray it gold, being sure to cover the back, too. Cut the tails of the bow into Vs before fixing it in place with hot glue; take the tails out to the sides and fix them with glue also. Another decorative option is to paint the base gold first, then make the trimmings on this wreath more spacious. The texture of gold painted vines showing through the trimming is most attractive.

Romantic roses

This simple wreath is easy to make. The rose flowers are air dried, and the rose leaves have been dried using borax as a desiccant. Rose leaves tend to keep their colour well when dried in this way. I find that air dried rose leaves seem to become too crinkled and fragile to use. Hot glue was used to fix the roses and leaves in place, then several light coats of aerosol acrylic semi-gloss sealer were used to seal the wreath. If you wish you could omit the sealer; however, roses do fade faster than other flowers and the sealer seems to slow down this process slightly. I try not to hang rose wreaths, or generally any flower wreath, in full sunlight as it does fade dried flowers quickly.

Page 3

Sparkles for Christmas

An extravagant combination of ribbons, tree ornaments and baubles makes for a truly memorable Christmas wreath. I've combined several ribbons in gold and silver, each with their own texture. Some are transparent, others have a fine wire woven down each edge which makes it easy to hold a bow in the desired shape. Gold and silver can be difficult to combine, however I feel it works well here with the addition of a pearl-white ribbon mingled amongst the other trimmings. Silver painted leaves plus gold metallic miniature bells and French horns add to the splendour. The bows are all tied first, then glued to the wreath base with hot glue. Be sure to trim the tails of the bows into Vs.

Beachcomber's holiday

Shells and other finds have been grouped onto this plain, bleached cane wreath base. I felt the lightness of the wreath's colour complemented the soft colours of the shells and driftwood. Some of these shells are quite heavy, and even though I was generous in my application of hot glue, I needed to support the shells while the glue was drying. As these are big shells, and quite varied in their shape and texture, I planned the design first by laying out the shells and driftwood in a circle and arranging them until I was pleased with the composition. It was then easy to transfer them to the wreath base. I feel it is important not to crowd the trimmings on this wreath, as the light cane base is definitely a design element in its own right. Another completely different alternative is to cover the wreath base with shells of the same species. I have shells called pippies in mind – they're the small clam-like shells that live in the sand on beaches. These are often marked in pretty patterns, and have a colour range through pinks, yellows, greys and purples. Simply mass them onto the wreath at different angles, fixing them in place with a dab of hot glue. You may like to seal shell-covered wreaths with a few coats of matt sealer. This will enhance the colours of the shells without adding any unnecessary shine.

Page 4

Autumn Pickings

There was nothing purchased to trim this wreath. The leaves are from the large box trees that line many streets, and the dried poppy heads came from a friend's garden. The nuts were in the pantry, though gathered nuts and pods could easily be substituted. The bundles of twigs were gathered from the garden and the long curly tendrils were clipped from my grapevine. All in all, a low-cost wreath! The attractiveness of this wreath lies in its varied textures, and the similarity of colours in the trimmings. Smooth leaves combine with the knotty twigs and grained nuts, and the unexpected shapes of poppy heads add dimension and yet another texture. The twigs were tied together into bundles with a strand of raffia (you could use scrap twine) and then trimmed to have even ends. The base is made from twisted grapevines, and the wreath has been sprayed with two coats of matt sealer to add lustre rather than shine.

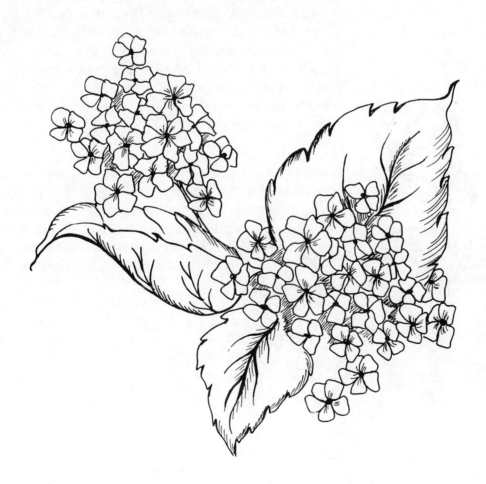

Page 5

A garland for the bride

These silk roses have had their petals stiffened with a product made to stiffen fabric for use in various crafts. There are several products available, and your craft shop will advise you about fabric stiffeners. The process of stiffening your roses starts with the removal of the flower from the stem. Pour some stiffening solution into a bowl and start to rub the thick, milky substance into each petal of the flowers. Rub this well into each side of the petals before setting the flower aside to dry. Sometimes it is necessary to bundle together little wads of kitchen plastic and push these between the petals to hold them in position while drying. The plastic is easily removed when the flower is dry. The flower will be lighter in colour when dry. The manufacturers of fabric stiffener suggest that you spray or paint your dry flowers with white acrylic paint, prior to painting with another colour. However, I liked the result of simply using white paint, as the soft glow of the original silk colour showed through, giving the flowers a peachy pink tint. I sprayed the vine wreath base with white acrylic paint, then glued the roses around it using hot glue. Dried pyrethrum daisies were mingled around the roses, leaving the vine base to show through in parts. I like the idea of a floral wreath decorating the front door of the bride's home – there it becomes the symbol of happy events about to occur!

Page 6

Nursery friends – two simple wreaths

A vine base was painted with two coats of 'Country Blue' acrylic paint. I've then grouped some dried, strong-stemmed yellow flowers and wired them together, adding red and white gingham ribbon bows to cover the wire. I've fixed these five posies (an odd number always looks best) around the wreath with hot glue. The charm of this wreath is in the strong colours used, and the simple style of the trimming.

For the Teddy Bear Wreath, I suggest you wind your tape measure around a bleached cane wreath base to ascertain the length of the fabric strip needed to trim the wreath. Do the same for the bow by tying the tape measure into a bow that is in proportion to the wreath. Add these two measurements together and cut a strip of fabric about 12 cm (4³/₄″) wide by the required length. Fold the strip over with right sides facing and stitch down the long side. Cut off the length needed for the bow, cut the ends of the bow strip at an angle then stitch across. Unpick a few stitches in the middle of the long edge, and turn right side out.

The remainder of the fabric strip will be wound around the wreath. Turn the wreath strip to the right side, and press neatly. Overcast the raw edges of the narrow ends with hand or machine stitching. Wind the strip around the wreath base, starting on the wrong side of the wreath and securing the start and finish with hot glue. Tie the bow and glue it to the top of the wreath. Add teddy bear refrigerator magnets, or small fabric bears, or painted bear cut-outs to each wind of the fabric, securing them with hot glue.

47

Page 7

Flowers with sphagnum moss

This charming country-style wreath is very simple to make. The greenery is wound onto the green painted vine base using a medium gauge wire. I selected variegated leafy foliage, and dried it in borax (see Drying plants using desiccants). The daisies were also dried in borax. Some air dried love-in-the-mist flowers (they look more like pods!) were added amongst the foliage because I liked their fluffy texture and they added another tone of green. Sphagnum moss, which is a greenish-white colour, was added in clumps, and also wired into place. The moss added softness, and its intriguing texture was a welcome addition. The daisies, being in short supply at the time, were more or less spaced evenly around the wreath and glued, tucking their stems down into the foliage. When you're considering a wreath of one predominant colour, and there is the risk of your base showing through, I suggest you first paint the wreath base in a soft shade of the chosen colour.

Wheat with plaited raffia

Simple country charm that is easily achieved using only one colour. The wreath base is bleached willow, and the differing textures of raffia and wheat are a good contrast. Wrap some loose strands of raffia around, like a ribbon, securing the ends at the back of the wreath with hot glue. Group three bunches of four pieces of raffia for plaiting. Plait a long length of raffia, then wrap it around the wreath, first one way, then the other, to create a crisscross effect, again securing ends with hot glue. When the strands become thin during plaiting, as they will, for raffia pieces are always variable in length, simply overlap more pieces onto the thinning strand and continue plaiting. When the plait is the correct length, trim the raffia ends. At the lower front of the wreath, wheat has been glued to fan outwards from the centre, and more loops of plaited and unplaited raffia bows have been placed amongst the wheat. To complete, tie about 15 pieces of raffia into a well shaped bow with evenly clipped ends and glue it to the centre of the wheat.

Page 8

A bouquet swag

These are a lovely alternative to wreaths, and are particularly easy to make. Lay the longest flower stalks down first, then gradually lay down the shorter stalks until the spray is complete. I find it easier to hold the ends firmly in my left hand while adding more flowers with the right. This may not be easy for some, so if this is the case I suggest you try laying the stalks down on some flat surface, then gathering them up when complete. Tie the stalks together, or wire them for extra strength. Group together a bunch of wheat stalks and trim the ends evenly. Lay these around the previous tie, and tie firmly into place with wire, adding a long hanging loop at the back. These stalks add design impact and hide the inevitable uneven stem lengths of the flowers. Add a wide coconut fibre ribbon bow (sinimay ribbon) to complete the swag. This form of swag looks lovely at Christmas time. Small sprays of holly, pine or mistletoe tied together with large tartan, red or green ribbons and placed on doors, mirrors, or, in cold climates, outside on the gatepost.

Waxed fruit with flowers in a vertical swag

The process of making this dramatic decoration is really quite simple. Its only drawback is that the materials could become expensive. All the fruit and flowers are wound onto a length of plaited raffia. Decide where you wish to hang the swag and how long it needs to be, then make a strong length of plaited raffia for a base, or use nylon rope or plastic bags bound together. Starting at the lowest point, wind on the trimmings using a medium gauge wire. The assortment of trimmings on my swag is really enormous, as I used up leftovers from previous wreaths and swags. The colours and textures are varied, and I have tucked in sphagnum moss to add extra texture. It all seems to go together surprisingly well! Continue winding until you have covered the base, leaving enough to bind on wheat stems and a ribbon bow as for the Bouquet Swag. Be sure you cover the sides adequately, but leave the back flat so that it will sit flush with the wall. This method of making a long, vertical swag can be applied in many circumstances, using only

49

one form of trimming if necessary. They would be charming as wedding decorations, or hanging either side of doors, down the sides of cupboards, above a small table, on doors, mirrors – the list goes on. Using only one trim, such as variagated foliage, or only one type of flower can look simply wonderful, and often dramatic.

A small dried flower swag

The curved base can be made from any wreath base material discussed earlier in the book. I've known swag makers to cut a wreath base in half, binding the raw ends of the fibres, thus creating two half-circle swag bases. Tie wire or strong raffia around each raw end and create hanging loops through which ribbons can pass. Start winding on flowers from the centre using medium gauge wire, and working upwards until you reach the ends. Return to the centre and fill in the space with more flowers, gluing some stems at the back so that they fill in and continue to give the curved appearance the swag needs, rather than making a V shape. Tie the swag to a bedhead or bedstead, or to wall hooks, using long ribbons passed through the hanging loops then tied into bows. This can be a charming decoration in a child's room, especially for feminine little girls.

Credits

Thank you to C & S Imports in Melbourne (Just Craft Shops in Sydney and Melbourne) for the dried flowers, raffia and wreath bases; Offray ribbons for their cut-edge, wire edge and polyester ribbons; Janet Wong from Liberon Waxes in Sydney for waxed fruit and flowers; sphagnum moss is available through Tonia Todman Craft Kits.

For information about craft kits and materials available from Tonia Todman, please write to:

Tonia Todman Craft Kits
PO Box 12
Balmain NSW 2041

Notes